THE BOOK OF AL

The Story of a Psychiatric Survivor, Me

Allan Jones

Order this book online at www.trafford.com
or email orders@trafford.com

Most Trafford titles are also available at major online book retailers.

© Copyright 2013 Allan Jones.
All rights reserved. No part of this publication may be reproduced,
stored in a retrieval system, or transmitted, in any form or by
any means, electronic, mechanical, photocopying, recording, or
otherwise, without the written prior permission of the author.

Names have been changed to protect the privacy of those in this story.

Printed in the United States of America.

ISBN: 978-1-4669-8358-8 (sc)
ISBN: 978-1-4669-8357-1 (e)

Trafford rev. 03/11/2013

 www.trafford.com

North America & international
toll-free: 1 888 232 4444 (USA & Canada)
phone: 250 383 6864 ♦ fax: 812 355 4082

To my daughters, who I love

Insanity: doing the same thing over and over again and expecting different results.

—Albert Einstein

My name is Allan Jones. I was born July 12, 1958. Where do I start?

I come from a small family. My older brother Danny was seven years older than me. Lynn was seven years younger and Bobby was 14 years younger than me. Here, I sit in my room at Apartment Number Two, staring at my blank screen of my P-200 Toshiba laptop computer wondering and wondering what my life has become.

I would like to talk about living with mental illness. At the age of 13, I was diagnosed with schizophrenia. I did not understand anything. How could a young child of 13 years of age understand what it meant to have schizophrenia?

That year, I spent six months at the Triple Trees Sanatorium. When my dad left me at the hospital, I said "Dad, I do not want to stay here. I want to go back home with you."

I was unable to complete Grade 8 that year. During my school years, I had told my classmates that I felt like an outcast. I felt as if I did not belong. I became a loner. I didn't know day in and day out in Grade 8 what my life was going to turn out to be. It is hard when you come from kindergarten to Grade 8 with all these kids who are supposed to be your friends and all of a sudden they turn their backs on you. I was alone, suffering from insomnia and depression, even though I was diagnosed with schizophrenia by Dr. Smart.

It does not sound like the proper diagnosis, but years later it became clear to me that it was. In school, I had been the class clown. I loved making people laugh—teachers and students alike. Yes, yes, those were the good old days. I thought they would never end. But in Grade 8 I struggled and struggled trying to keep it all together, but it all fell to the wayside. I couldn't get out of bed anymore. I didn't want to eat. I was angry at the fact that nothing seemed to be going right. Mom was in the hospital with post-partum depression, Dad was working and trying his best to keep it all together. My grandmother was taking care of my new brother, Bobby.

I loved my father; he was a good man, a dedicated husband and a dedicated worker. I loved my mom too, but it was hard when I was 13. When brother Bobby, the youngest, was born, my mother suffered from post-partum depression, as she did with my birth, as well. My poor dad thought he was going to lose his mind from the pressure. I recall him saying year later, "When you and your mom were sick, I felt like high-tailing it to the hills." But J.N. Jones, my father, did not high-tail it to the hills. He stood by his family, supported each and every one of us. I will tell you more about him later on.

Before this time, I was a good student, average and attentive. I did my homework, socialized and had fun. I remember Miss Rain, my Grade 6 teacher. We had hot dog sales and dessert sales to save up money to go from Normalville to Large Town, to Miss Rain's parents' place. It was a great time in Grade 6. How I loved the girls! I had some sweethearts, but as most boys are, I was shy.

The guys in my class stuck to playing sports, the girls played hopscotch, and together we played TV tag. I only remember bits and pieces of the earlier grades. Once, in Kindergarten, I had goose bumps so I asked my friend about them. He said, "That is not chicken pox." So I went up to the teacher, Mrs. Witty, and said, "I do not feel well. I think I have chicken pox." She said, "No, you probably only have goose bumps because you are cold."

A year or two later, they showed us how to use the telephone, a great instrument at that time. Now I am 54 years of age; it was quite the invention back then. I always thought, *What if Alexander Graham Bell's name was Alexander Graham Siren? Instead of the ringing, it would be a siren.* That was a line from a comedian.

Mr. Correct was my Grade 8 teacher. He was a good guy. The school I attended was the Saint Peter's Grade School. I was versed in the Bible and we held mass in the gym, then later across the road at Saint Peter's Parish in Ronnal once the church was built. I was brought up a Roman Catholic, baptized with godparents. My godparents were my aunt and uncle on my mom's side; I remember them to be lovely people.

In Grade 8 the first time around, my friends deserted me. These were the people I trusted for nine years and they turned their backs on me. I wondered, *Why would they do that?* How could they reject me, criticize me and ridicule me, always make fun of me? Before I was hospitalized, they laughed at my jokes and my clowning around and then they just disowned me. I was all alone, all alone, all alone! It was so scary. I could not believe it.

My parents knew that I was falling back. They started to take me to the doctors and after about two months I was admitted to the Triple Trees hospital. Prior to being a mental institution, the Triple Trees was a tuberculosis hospital that was opened by Dr. Tests. When tuberculosis was finally eradicated they turned it into a mental health facility. When you are a child of 13 years of age, you do not realize what an asylum is, but I found out quickly what it was all about. Can you imagine being put on a ward where they have quiet rooms? Rooms to put in people who lose control and lock the door on them in hopes that they can cool down? Doors that just have a small window for staff to observe the patient? It was bizarre.

So there I was at Normalville's Triple Trees hospital with its quiet rooms, its common area, its TV room and its bedrooms. I remember my dad walking away, after dropping me off. I said,

"Dad, do not leave me here." He said, "I am sorry son, I have to."

The next morning came early, and I did not sleep well. I got out of the bed and started walking into that ward, past the hallways, past the common room and then finally to the staff room. There was G.M., a long-haired university student. He was tall, slender and kind-looking. He just looked at me and asked, "How are you?" I looked at him and said, "I do not know."

Yes, the staff. Oh, if I could remember all their names. Mrs. Care was great then. There was Miss Bright, she was fantastic, too. She still works at the same hospital. Then there was Mrs. Rann, she was an African-Canadian.

I would spend six months there, not being able to go to school, unable to see my parents. Six months of intensive treatment, and then again in the late 1960s and again in the early 1970s. It was a strange place and it felt foreign to me.

* * *

I had a normal upbringing. I had an older brother Danny who used to do some pretty sadistic stuff to me. What a prankster! He stuck me in the buttocks with a hatpin, which hurt! Shot a pellet gun at me, using unripened blueberries as projectiles. Scared me half to death in the wilderness when it was winter by pushing me over a cliff with my toboggan. I was buried head-first. When I pulled my head out of the snowbank, he said to me, "The wolves are coming to get you." Ah, too many memories to go through! I laugh when I think of those times.

Then there was Lynn, my younger sister, by seven years. She was OK. I followed Danny's ways and tried to razz her, but not as much as Danny had done to me.

I was born and raised in Hill Top at 3461 Captain Road, on the highway, about ten minutes from Normalville. I was not that good in sports. I found that basketballs were too hard to dribble. Floor hockey wasn't that bad. But I was a good goalie in hockey and soccer and a decent defenseman in flag football. It was a good thing that my father had a steady job with MEN Mines. I was able to hang out with all the same people, as compared to other families who had to move around a lot. Unlike them, we lived in the same home during my entire childhood. That was a good thing. I do not know how military families do it. They are always on the go.

When I was 11, I put together a motorcycle. It was a Suzuki K-11 that my dad had bought for me. It took two years to bring it to shape because it was a basket case. I rebuilt it and I discovered my love for mechanics.

The girls around Hill Top, boy, we had some beauties! I always looked at Normalville as a wonderful place for beautiful women. I guess the reason is that working miners and hardworking housewives produce good-looking, healthy women. My first love was Cindy. I was about 12 years old and she was 13. She was a year older and Ukrainian. What a beauty she was. She was so beautiful, but I was too shy to give her that first kiss. But I should have! That is what shyness did to a boy like me.

* * *

I am telling this story by dictation on a brand new Sony dictaphone tape recorder that I bought just to write this book. Also being used is a voice recognition program on my laptop computer. We will see how well it works. It is my life story and I hope that you enjoy it.

* * *

Times were different during my first stay at the hospital. They did not have many antipsychotics back then. (I remember taking the drug Largactil, known generically as clorpromazine.) So one thing for sure was that we got a lot of exercise at Triple Trees. We would walk from the hospital all the way to Learn-A-Lot University and back. It was great! I loved going to the university, walking in those big corridors and seeing the tower where all the library books were held. It was such a treat. Oh, and the winters were bitterly cold for those walks.

I was never put in one of those quiet rooms and it was a good thing because some of the other child patients were. All of us ranged in age from six to 13. Reg was about seven and he was autistic. Baara was a black girl, about eight years old; she was blind. Garran was about 8; well, he had epileptic seizures, which I saw. Young Ryan would clap his hands together and he would thumb through books with much excitement. I do not know what his diagnosis was. Then there was Big Dennis and he was really messed up. On one of our outings from the hospital to the downtown shopping centre, he went into stores and lifted stuff. Then there was Damon: he was my best friend. He was not as severely disabled as the others or myself. Oh, I should not forget about Patricia. That was love at first sight. Patricia was just a young girl, the same age that I was, 13. She had nice long brown hair. One thing about Patricia: I could never figure out was what her problem was why she was there.

Now it is time to meet some more of the staff. There was G.M. and B.M., they were twin brothers. B.M. did not work at the hospital but G.M. did. What they used to do with me is we would go down to the billiards hall in the old part of town and shoot a lot of pool. I learned how to play snooker pretty proficiently. The twins had long hair parted in the middle and I said to myself, "I am going to grow my hair long and part it in the middle, too." And, later, I did.

My favorite show, which I liked to watch in the TV room, was "Emergency". It was about two guys in a fire department who were paramedics;

it was before the time of paramedics today. I also enjoyed watching "Spiderman". It was my favorite little cartoon.

Sometimes I wonder, you know, with my mom's post-partum depression, if something left traces of illness on me as an unborn child or as an infant and whether or not that has anything to do directly with my mental health. (At first you might wonder, *Well, he jumps from this to that, to that to this, but it will all come out in the end?* Keep reading. There's still some wild stuff ahead.)

It was a nice, bitter walk to Learn-A-Lot University and afterwards we would go back to the hospital and have some hot chocolate and marshmallows. Damon and I liked to play card games with the staff, Crazy Eights and Rummy Five-Hundred. I remember one of Damon's questions to the staff, "Will I have to go to the special school here on site at the hospital?" And the doctors told him, "No, you will not have to, Damon, because you are much higher-functioning than that. That is for people who are developmentally delayed." What Damon wanted most was to be a goalie for the Normalville Warriors.

When Christmastime came around, Damon would not open his presents with the other kids. He saved his presents until he would be home with his family once more. It is hard when you are put in a place like that and you cannot even see your parents. It is pretty sad. It is sort of strange, you know. I had parents that I was not allowed to see for six months, but some of those other children had no parents to speak of at all. Some had been left there.

Oh, one of the other staff members was Dallas. He was a big muscular guy, with long curly hair down to his waistline. You would not want to mess with him but he was cool, I mean super-cool.

One of the strange, surreal things that happened at the hospital was when Miss Bright, who still works there, showed me the morgue. It was a TB hospital, as I said before, and that is what that morgue had been used for. *At least I am only mentally ill,* I thought, *and did not have tuberculosis.*

Now, back to Baara, the little black girl. I remember having a little portable radio and when Sammy Davis Jr. came on with the "Candy Man Can" song came on, how I loved it when

Baara would start turning around and singing, "And the candy man can."

As for Garran with his epilepsy, I had seen one of his convulsions and I could not believe what I was witnessing, how a young child like that was trying to swallow his tongue and his eyeballs went back into his head. They would have to put something in there to stop him from chewing on his tongue, as he was vibrating and shaking. It is one of the most horrible things you can ever see. Poor, poor Garran.

Then there was young Ryan with his flipping through pages of books and rocking back and forth to get some sort of comfort.

Then there was Reg, who said nothing at all.

Another one of the staff when I was 13, his name was Mr. Dare. He was hilarious, I am telling you, what a comedian! I liked him and his humour. I remember Damon and Mr. Dare playing hockey on the rink outside the hospital, when Mr. Dare slipped and bumped the back of his head on the ice. He was OK.

One day, Mrs. Care, a nurse, took all of us to her father's cottage. It was winter, it was a beautiful winter, and we went camping and stayed in one of the camps. It was weird, though.

I remember G.M. taking young Ryan, and forcing him to run through the wintry water, snow, and slush without any boots on. It is unfortunate to say but sometimes, I guess, when you are dealing with a developmentally challenged individual, it is possible to lose control and take it out on the poor patient, but that is totally wrong.

With Miss Bright we all went sliding, and poor Miss Bright! She lost control of the toboggan and smashed into a tree right between her legs. What a mess that was. It is a good thing she did not hurt herself too badly.

Yes, on the way back to town from the cottage, there was a big storm brewing. In the country where we were, the snow was coming down like crazy and the wind was blowing. Mrs. Care had a blue station wagon (I believe it was a Chevy) and she was a good driver because she made it up the long hills and corners. She knew exactly how to feed the accelerator to make sure that we would not be stranded, and we managed to make it back to the Triple Trees all in one piece. Poor Mrs. Care hurt her ankle getting out of the car or something, and asked for Damon to come and help her.

I also remember Mrs. Rann, my nurse during that time. Once, I had flu-like symptoms and I was quite ill, to put it lightly. She stayed with me by my side, one-on-one. It took a couple of days until I was better.

Another time, Dallas took Damond and I out to Skylight auditorium to watch the movie "Woodstock" and it was great! Mr. Dallas also took Damond and I to see the first show of the movie "Billy Jack". My favorite song back then was "The Lion Sleeps Tonight"—"In the jungle, the mighty jungle, the lion sleeps tonight."

So that was my first encounter with the Triple Trees Sanatorium.

I forgot to mention, my parents did come to see me at almost the end of my six-month stay. Danny, my older brother, was crying in the elevator when they left.

Despite this, something wonderful had happened when Danny, my mom and my dad were there. Reg, the child who had autism, jumped on Danny's back and said to him, "Dad, wasn't that amazing!?" That was the first time that Reg had ever spoken.

* * *

So back to school I go with Mr. Correct, my teacher in Grade 8. Half-days at home, half-days at school. In the mornings, I worked on the little Ford Cortina car by sanding it and painting it and changing the brake shoes, changing all of those parts. I loved mechanics back then. My dad did the best he could to teach me all he knew.

Oh, it was so sad. The other students I spent so many years with in elementary school had sort of brushed me off. You know how the pecking order is. You know, if there is something that a student does not like about another student, they go after them. Yes, the pecking order.

Before my first admission at age 13, what had transpired is that Danny, my older brother, married his first love, because she was with child. They moved in with us. It was very stressful for all of our family with Danny not being able to complete high school and getting married to his love and sharing our two-bedroom house with his love. There were a lot of people in the house, and my mom, also pregnant, did not see eye-to-eye at times with Danny's wife. Soon, Gary came around, their first-born. I remember accusing my brother Danny, "You have stolen my bed." What a wrong thing to say. How heartless I was by saying that. Just to show the human condition, the way we look upon things, the way we look at things can be unfair.

So I was now back at home and going back to school in Grade 8 with the kids I grew up with. I was sort of isolated; no one had much to say to me anymore. Danny and his wife were in their own place. My older brother, my protector, was gone. It was so unfortunate but, least to say, I failed my Grade 8. I had to take it over again, which I did.

So at 13, I had ended up in the hospital. But the thing was, I thought that everything would be all right. I turned 14 and finished up Grade 8, the full year. Then I started high school.

I only went to one high school dance. I wore a gold medallion of a wolf around my neck. That was a good memory.

I was very popular in gym. I was known for my strength. Once, I was on the trampoline when I bounced a couple of times and bounced off. I got my head stuck in between the springs and fell off. All the kids were calling me Trampoline Fred. My basketball playing was not very good. I could dribble a little, but was sort of comical to watch and they called me The Six Million Dollar Man, which was a popular show back then. I guess it was because of the way I ran.

Being naïve and young, I wasn't prepared for some of the dangers of life, and at 15 years of age, I was sexually assaulted by an employer, by the name of E. Pedophile. What a mess that was.

Yes, I was supposed to go to Large Town with him. He had a fruit market down where I lived. One of the friends I grew up with said that E. Pedophile needed someone's help to pick up the fruit and vegetables in Large Town, four hours away. My friend could not help him that evening. So my friend called me up and asked if I wanted to go.

So here we are, me and E. Pedophile, an older guy, a bigger guy, driving at midnight. I am only 15, remember, I am not a man yet. We stopped at the Whales Pool aquarium, halfway between Normalville and Large Town, near Halfland and Ortim. He stopped the truck.

He says to me, "Well, I have to go to the washroom."

So I said, "Well, OK, go to the washroom."

He got out of the truck and, instead, he walked over to the passenger side of the truck where I was and he opened the door. "Take off your pants."

I did not know what to do. I had a knife in my pocket and there was a fire extinguisher in the truck. What should I do, smash him in the head with the fire extinguisher, pull out my knife and stab him? I was scared. I had never been accosted like that before. So I took my pants off. He climbed into the truck.

You have to consider this is 3:00 a.m. in the morning. When I tried to run away from the truck, he jumped back in and tried to run me over. I tripped because my pants were down. I finally made it to the ditch and rolled in it so he could not get me, and he took off like mad. This was at the Whales Pool and I went to the back of the building and I yelled because there were people living there. I yelled, "Help me, help me, I have just been raped!"

The Ontario Provincial Police arrived there very quickly. I remember one of the officers telling me, "We are going to get that fancy pants, son."

So the police took me to the hospital to get a swab test. My dad had to drive from Normalville to Ortim to pick me up. I was a mess. I did not know how to act. I did not cry. My dad was silent.

Anyway, we had to go to court in Ortim. The judge gave the guy two months in a psychiatric facility to determine whether or not he was a homosexual. My point of view on all of this is that the guy is a child molester, not a homosexual.

Well, needless to say, that messed up my high school plans. I ended up back in the Triple Trees Sanatorium. It was bad this time. I was suffering from a really bad depression. Unlike the first episode at age 13, I was older and I understood more about mental illness. I knew that I was mostly dealing with depression and insomnia. That meant back to the hospital for another six months and not being able to see my parents again.

I was first put in the Kind Care Hospital, which is now called the Saint Francis Hospital, where they administered electric shock treatment, ECT. I had a series of eight shock treatments at 15 years of age, in order to rid me of my supposed schizophrenia which, at the time, they really did not know anything about. After three weeks, my parents brought me to Triple Trees for rehabilitation. Maybe it was the shock treatment that put me into a state of confusion or alienation or whatever, but I was pretty messed up.

While at the Kind Care Hospital, I used to phone the Green family, the family of a friend, and say things like "Your dad is here", reason being there was a man who looked like Mr. Green. They asked me why I was doing this to them. Pretty bizarre. I apologized when I had my feet back on the ground.

When I was transferred to Triple Trees, I remember not having a decent bowel movement, so they administered an enema. I cannot remember the nurse's name, but for some reason I called her a witch. I guess the procedure was uncomfortable and, at 15, with all this going on, I guess people say things they do not mean.

It was all different this time. Different staff with new implementations and I was one of the first on board. I do not remember all of the staff, but there was Randel, with the long hair. Also Timothy, another staffperson, who was in the army. As for some of the kids, there was Marilyn, who was beautiful, K.K. my roommate (what a messed up person he was), and B.J., a girl. And then there was Patricia, who was the girl that I was in there with when I was 13. She was in with the adolescents, like I was. Lastly, there was Laina. She was tall and blonde and I think that she had been mistreated, and that is why she was there.

I was severely depressed with severe insomnia, and an outcast of the world. The assault kept running through my mind. At 15, what are you to do in such a situation? It still runs through my mind now at 54 years of age. I blamed myself for things I had no control of.

I was always a happy-go-lucky kid, with a good sense of humor. However, age really hardens a person when you discover what life is really all about.

I just have to get this off my chest. My roommate was K.K. I should have told the staff that I wanted a different roommate. The reason being, he made sexual advances towards me. So one day I put him in a headlock. I did not hit him, I just choked him out a bit and told him to leave me alone. I did not want any part of it.

Then there was Marilyn. What a beautiful 16-year-old girl, but she was something else. I was a little younger. Unfortunately, I found out years later from a staff member for the adolescent unit that Marilyn had been murdered. That made me feel bad because she was so understanding and gorgeous. I think she was put in the Triple Trees hospital because she stole a car. Maybe she had to do some probation, I do not know. The thing with Marilyn is that one night she smashed a glass bottle of milk and slit her wrists with it. I remember saying to her, "Dear, do not do that, do not do that!" So I ran to Timothy and said, "Marilyn is hurting herself." He ran in and took her to the Kind Care Hospital to get stitches. When they returned, instead of sitting and talking to her, they put her in the quiet room in the children's ward. I am going to let it go at that.

* * *

In 1974, I was done at McDonald High School in Ronnal. I completed Grade 9 with three credits. Everyone knew about the incident with E. Pedophile and I was ridiculed some more. You would think that there would be more maturity and understanding.

Some of the neighborhood kids always called me down, called me a goof and told me to get lost and, basically, didn't want anything to do with me. I was isolated again. They all knew about the incident with E. Pedophile. It destroyed my life in a way that I could not understand. It was not my fault. I did not do it willingly and I was fighting for my life. I needed more than just counseling and admittance to the Triple Trees at that time. I wished someone could wave a magic wand and take all the pain away.

One teacher, Miss Tall, told me not to quit school at 16, but I ended up quitting anyway. It was tough to go to work. I found a job pumping gas for a few months and then moved on to a carwash for a while. These were the jobs that were offered in Normalville, before you got offered work mining at MEN or Big Mountain mine.

Finally, at 17 or 18 years old, my depression and insomnia lifted and I began to relive my life. I tried to make a go of it in Saskatchewan for a bit, but I came back and worked with my older brother Danny paving driveways for a bit. That was hard work but I had to do it. Who would hire someone without their Grade 12 education? Only manual labor was available.

The people I worked with were all drinkers and I got into drinking myself. It was OK at the time because I was not in a relationship. I was not married and my brother was a truck driver. On the weekends we would binge drink and every Friday we would suck back a few browns. That was the extent of my life back then.

Then, at age 18, I finally got a break. I was on unemployment insurance and I had the opportunity to upgrade to my Grade 10 at High End College. Then I took the heavy duty equipment mechanics program. That was 10 months' long, and I pursued my career as a diesel mechanic from 1977 to 1979. I worked for a company down south in Steel Town named L & L repairs for seven months. I moved there with Danny and his girlfriend.

It was all right, and I was learning a lot of interesting things. My associations and friendships were good and I had a good time with the people there. To put it simply, I felt very good. I felt like I was going somewhere. I did get in trouble with the law when I was charged with impaired driving, but did not receive any penalties as it was only my first offence. I should have taken more care with regard to the drinking. I wonder if I was self-medicating with the booze and marijuana at the time, whether my mental illness simply lay dormant for a while?

My employers were good people and I adapted to Steel Town, Ontario quite well. I lived in the same apartment building as my older brother Danny. I made friends with his friends and all was good. Before I moved to Steel Town with Danny, my relationship with him was significant. Despite the age difference, we were good friends. We were not the best of people. We were heavy duty I guess with the drinking and smoking up. People get carried away with things they should not do. It is part of growing up. No one can say that they do not have experiences. Back in the 1970s, laws were more lenient and impaired driving was not looked at as badly as it is nowadays but it is serious. Life brings you different challenges. A person has to experience things. We experienced a lot.

It was party time at 19 years of age, for I was a real free spirit. Then there were the women. Reanna was beautiful; so was Suze, but she was just interested in getting pregnant. Suze was Randy's daughter. Randy, my boss, was married for the second time to Reanna. Suze was adorable but all she wanted was kids and I was not ready for that so we did not pursue it.

I spent approximately seven months out there fixing up machinery. When I left Steel Town to return to Normalville, I started working at Large Machines & Equipment in Larson in 1980. They really showed me a lot about the trade. I worked hard but I was not a registered mechanic. I thought I was, but it turned out Randy had made a mess of that by offering me a wage subsidy. He convinced me that it was an apprenticeship in diesel mechanics, but it wasn't. Nowadays you cannot do that sort of thing. I spent a couple of years with Large Machines and, although it was a small outfit, we worked on big contracts like Caterpillar. I made friends, continued my drinking and smoking some pot, and worked in different departments. I worked on heavy equipment and in parts and small engine. I tried sales once in a while. Two to three years went by. I loved those people but I had to say goodbye. My foreman was a real redneck. He and I never saw eye-to-eye, which was unfortunate because I was young and I should have been instructed in mechanics but I did not get the direction. I had tears when I resigned because there were a lot of people there that I cared for. I went to the Unemployment Insurance office and applied at the Radar Base in Normalville, Ontario.

In 1982, I was hired upon my interview on a six-month contract at the Radar Base as a civilian working for National Security. I was building large diesel engines called automatic power units, or APU's. If the hydro went out, the base would have to depend on an internal power unit. I enjoyed it there and they paid well.

Two years before, in 1980 I had married my Roxanne and she was the reason why I worked as hard as I could. I met Roxanne in a unique way. While I was working at Large Machines, I was living at the Eagle Eye Hotel. I went around Larson and I found a basement apartment. As luck would happen, Roxanne lived in the same house with her parents, her sister and her brother. Times were good and there was employment to be found. Roxanne and I had pizza every night from Pizza Pit. We did a bit of a drinking and some pot-smoking. We did not have children at this time as we wanted to enjoy ourselves. We were married for 25 years. I will explain later what became of us.

Back to my job at the radar base. I liked it, but Normalville hit some hard times, so my contract was not renewed. I applied at Big Mountain Mine, but they were on strike and they were not hiring.

Soon after my employment at the Radar Base ended in 1982, I lost my brother Danny. It was really hard on me. He allegedly committed suicide with a shotgun and I could not understand why. I was in Normalville and he was still in Steel Town. My mother called me to inform me and she said, "You have to be strong for us, Allan, because Danny, your brother, shot himself."

I did not know how to handle it emotionally and I did not know how to react. It is so strange. There is a wide spectrum of emotions and I remember starting to laugh and then I cried.

My family went to Steel Town. The police wanted to see us. My parents were so rattled that I took charge. I was used to driving in the big cities, so I drove them there. My dad wanted to leave Danny there and let Welfare handle it, but I told my dad that we could not leave him in the cement jungle. When we got there, we rented a hotel room and the next day we went to the police station and spoke to the trauma officer. He told us that it was ruled as a suicide. I asked if we could bring the shotgun back with us but they thought it would tear my mother's heart out, and I agreed. One of the officers bought it for his collection, I would assume.

One of the detectives was belligerent toward me and asked if I wanted to come to the morgue in order to see my dead brother. I sarcastically said, "Sure," but we did not go and that was a good thing.

Was it a suicide or a homicide? Only God knows. I was told that Danny had used a fishing rod to activate the trigger on the shotgun. He blew away the right side of his heart and the left side of his right lung and he remained alive throughout the admittance to the hospital where he told the doctors to let him die. He did not have much in his apartment, except his waterbed and a few other things. He had the songs called "House of the Rising Sun" and "If I had Jesse's Girl". I kept his chessboard made of maple wood and burned my name into it. That was all that was left of Danny.

It is hard when you lose a loved one in such a tragic circumstance. I loved my brother and I still have fond memories of him.

At about seventeen years of age, Danny had himself a Triumph Bonneville motorcycle 650 CC's with cross-over pipes—that means the exhaust pipes went over on the same side. We put shorty mufflers on it so it sounded really, really mean. It was all painted up, we had stripped it right down to nothing and built it right back up again. I was eleven years old, so this was pretty exciting stuff.

One of Danny's cars that we fixed up was a 1964 Plymouth Fury. It had a 383 Dodge engine in it. It was also equipped with a four-speed Hurst shifter and 4-11 racing gears in the rear-end. That is for the differential at the back, for people that are not technically inclined. I do not know how we made it, but we made a Ford engine fit inside there. I believe it may have been a 351 Cleveland, but I am not sure. I do not know how we mounted the bell housing to the engine and transmission but it all worked out.

Before all of that, Danny was working for Main Bay Wholesale, at that time fixing cigarette vending machines. They were quite mechanical, as opposed to what you have with digital vending machines today. He worked very hard there; he always worked hard at any job he had.

Tom and Jerry were Danny's best friends back then and they bought themselves a motorcycle that my father had fixed up. It was a 1957 Harley Davidson Knucklehead. It had tubular forks and six-foot exhaust pipes with a suicide stick for a gear shift. It was called a suicide stick because you would have to shift it while lifting one of your legs and just use your hand to shift the gears. I have to tell you, that was quite the machine.

Another vehicle that Danny owned was a 1969 Ford Falcon. It had a 289 V-8 engine and a smart engine-smart meaning, very clean cut. Just a decent engine, like mechanics say, a real plain Jane. You never figured a little car like that could be so powerful.

Unfortunately, one day, Danny was leaving work at The Big Grocery Store when somebody ran right into him. The police officer said to

Danny that he was lucky as he could have lost his leg. However, Danny's reflexes were so fast that he only had some minor bumps and bruises. That was his second motorcycle accident. His first one was with a Honda 150. You always have to start off small. You always have to start off somewhere. Anyways, that time, he and his friend G.R. had gotten into an accident. This woman pulled out right in front of them and they ended up flipping right over her hood. G.R. ended up having to get some pins in his leg, but Danny just had cuts and bruises.

Yup, another thing Danny did, like I said before, was shoveling asphalt. They were building the new Highway 96 North from Normalville to Ronnal, Happer and Capetown. He was in the back of a Ford half-ton truck that we used for paving. There were two 45-gallon drums in the box of the truck. One had diesel and the other one had gas. Anyways, he was messing around on a Friday night, drinking. Ray and Danny were sitting in the back of the box. Carl, Dan and Lloyd were in the front seat of the truck. Carl was driving. Danny lit a cigarette and KA-BOOM. He ignited the whole thing right on fire, and blew up the whole truck.

It was amazing that none of them got killed in there. Danny received the worst of the burns, second—and third-degree burns over 70 percent of his body, but he still pulled through that. He was one tough monkey. I remember us visiting him in the Intensive Care Unit and he said to our mom and dad, "It would take more than that to keep a Jones down."

Danny was never diagnosed with anything but I know that he had a really tough life. He was a strong man. Sometimes it can get to the best of us. Some people can find a way out of the pain, but some cannot. It is unfortunate. I wish he would have reached out. I wish he had phoned me that night: I would have rushed from Normalville to Steel Town to see him.

What a devastating blow to his young family. When his young sons heard of it they hid under their beds. Poor Sam and Joe.

This book has to be taken seriously. Suicide destroys families and friends alike. It may even cause post-traumatic stress disorder. It ruined my family. My dad blamed himself for buying Danny the shotgun. At the funeral, my mom told me to feel my brother's hair and how soft it was as he lay there in his coffin. So I rubbed his hair. I don't think they ever recovered from Danny's death.

* * *

It was seven years later. I moved over to Strongman construction company for two years after spending six months with Highwater Marine. I worked as a forklift mechanic. It was all going well and in 1989, Roxanne and I had our second daughter Lawanda. I was glad about that because I was healthy. When we had Melanie in 1986, I was going through so much. I was experiencing auditory hallucinations and insomnia. I will speak of that later.

As I was saying, Lawanda was born in 1989 and I was full of joy again just like when Melanie was born, but the circumstances were different due to my mental and physical situation. I love both of my beautiful girls.

Lawanda was just a baby at that time and Melanie was three years old. Melanie was something else. She'd drag one of her toys around, a Transformer-like toy. She called him 'Man'. Once, I brought Melanie out to All Wood Homes. I asked her if she wanted to hear a talking car. She said yes. So I opened the door to the car and the car said, "The door is ajar." She said, "The car talks, Dad!" Another time, I was working under the hood on a car engine and Melanie accidentally turned the key on. I had to move my hands away from the fan before they were caught. Roxanne and I had a big laugh about that.

With Lawanda, I used to love putting her on the merry-go-round at the playground. She was quite young then. She also loved swinging. Both of the girls were like me when I was young—happy-go-lucky.

We were never without food on the table. At the time, I was fixing Caterpillar and Mack trucks. I was sandblasting, doing electrical, painting, air-hammering, engine rebuilding, hydraulic overhauling and transmission box installations. I was never a proficient welder, but I could do the basics of it. I also worked for Tractor Trailer Trucking, doing brake shoes, electrical wiring and whatever needed to be done and whatever I was told to do. I also worked for a lot of people of German descent and they are very exacting.

Roxanne and I moved around Battle Sound a little. It was difficult to find a good place but I found a basement apartment in a house near my work. We spent about six months there, unable to secure another residence.

We kept going back and forth to bring all our stuff from Normalville to Battle Sound. We had to go where the jobs were, I made a lot of friends and the people were friendly. I knew the auto dealerships and auto suppliers and I worked my heart out.

I was drinking again. However, drinking makes people do things they would not normally do, and in 1989, I received my third impairment charge. I did not do much time for it and it was pretty straightforward. Back in 1989, the law was different in terms of impairment and I only had to serve my term on the weekends for 14 days. I was in the Battle Sound Jail and it was an experience that I will never forget because that is when I started having auditory hallucinations again. I know people might be thinking I deserved this, but there are people out there who have done worse. I have been abstinent from drinking and smoking marijuana for 20 years now or more. I am sorry for the things that I have done and I certainly have learned from my experiences.

After the incarceration, I had received my driver's license back but I was still in rough shape. I quit drinking then. I started going to the Lords Hall in Battle Sound and I met a lot of good people there. Through my experience, I believe that people of all religious denominations who believe in Christ will be saved.

After Lawanda was born, we had a pretty good time despite my incarceration for impaired driving. People make mistakes and do break the law and get incarcerated but you cannot be ignorant of the law. With experiences come life lessons.

Finally, Roxanne and I found a perfect house after six months on Valley Street, across from a graveyard.

* * *

At Strongman, the guys and I often joked around. We made a body out of coveralls and put it under a truck to make it look like the foreman, Devon, was stuck underneath. We even stuck his old cowboy boots into the pant legs to make it look like him. Peter, the president at the time, thought it was hilarious but Devon did not find it so funny. You have to keep up the humor. We were just working people and we had to keep it light at times.

Times were good, but my illness began to appear again. This time, I experienced psychosis for the first time. My first psychotic episode was intense. I was working at All Wood Homes and, normally, I would have to work graveyard shifts because of my day job at Strongman Trucking. This night, I was working on a water pump and I had the engine out of a Ford Ranger truck. Then, suddenly, the voices started. I thought it was the devil out in the bush. They were coming after me. I was very scared and anxious thinking that someone was going to kill me. It went on and on. The fear took over me so severely that I jumped on the large forklift and I drove it into the storage area where all the wood was. I got down on my knees and prayed to God. I was pretty well messed up after that. I went to the doctor for treatment. He put me on medication.

Our house on Valley Street was owned by an elderly man. He had to sell the house, so Roxanne and I moved to Madd Avenue. I continued to work but the episodes continued. While working at Strongman, my day job, my episodes were more severe and I was pushing myself too hard by working long hours. The life of a mechanic is very hard mentally and physically. I should not have chanced it due to my problems.

Unfortunately, I had to leave my job at Strongman. They kept the job open for me so that I was covered by my insurance plan. Maggie was a good friend of Roxanne. She was thirty years older than Roxanne. Maggie showed Roxanne how to do sugaring which is a knitting technique.

The insurance company put me on disability payments and they also gave us a payment of $10,000. With this we immediately went to buy a car, a 1998 Ford Taurus. It had low mileage and it was in great condition, that is to say it did not have the heck driven out of it. We had it for a number of years. This was during my decline and my full-blown mental illness.

* * *

I want people to know that I worked hard as a mechanic and that I was not a freeloader. I wanted to be responsible to my family and earn a living. I did not expect to be put on lifetime disability and would go back to work if I was well again. I am not looking for sympathy but for empathy. Without mental health, you cannot do much. It is not the drinking and the pot-smoking that deteriorated my mental health.

I never believed that I was a full-blown alcoholic or that I was a full-blown pot smoker. The heaviest that I got into was the drugs was when I was a teenager. I tried some of the street drugs, experimenting like most kids did. I am not saying that society did this to me and that I should be compensated for it. The issue is paranoid schizophrenia; it is horrible.

* * *

I haven't explained yet why I had to leave Strongman. I was still employed there when my friend Kevin came along. He was a good guy.

We smoked a lot of pot together, a lot of oil just to catch a buzz. I do not think there is anyone who has not thought of what it would be like to catch a buzz. That is how I used to relax on my weekends. Kevin was a permanent employee at the All Wood Homes. He told Roxanne that I was tape recording information about the bosses because I believed I was being mistreated. Kevin said that he and Roxanne had to do something.

Yes, I was paranoid. It wasn't the first time. Back in 1985 in Normalville, I was in jail for my second impaired charge. I was doing ninety days on weekends. During my jail time, there had been a big trial happening in Normalville. Some guys from Get Tough Penitentiary—mafia—were being tried for murder. The jail was going crazy. All the inmates were flipping out, worried about the place being bombed. My troubles started when I was told by inmates to bring in drugs. All I said was that there was no way. Then I had to fight. Then I got into a biker problems, from outside the jail. I actually had a gun aimed at me through one of the large, barred windows. Man, did that ever mess me up. I was just trying to do my time. The whole freakin' place was after me. I was paranoid, but it was not part of my illness.

It was the circumstances. Still to this day, I fear for my life.

My paranoid ideas of that time are constantly with me. I try my best to tell myself that if the bikers wanted to take me out they would have done it by now. Here I am now, in 2012, and I still have the same paranoid thoughts. I am still alive. Is it all just a delusion? No, I don't think so. Yes, at 17 years of age I hung out with some bikers, but I was not a member. I liked drinking with them, being a kid. I did know a few of them. If they had a beef with me they would have done me in or if they thought I was a rat or a freak they would have messed me up for sure. I am just a guy struggling with mental illness.

My voices have changed over the years depending on my social situation and changes in medications. It is very hard to describe. It is horrible to be scared like that all the time and to fear so many things. I fear other people that I am dealing with, such as other patients and staff. (The thing about psychiatric hospitals is that you can tell almost immediately which staff members you want to share things with pretty much within the first week of being there. Some staff are worth their weight in gold, while others do not seem to want to be there, maybe in part due to burn-out; I do not know.) I tend to distance myself and fear that I cannot tell people things because the voices tell me that those people are all part of the elaborate plan and they are out to get me. I have a rational voice and thinking as well. I know that the delusions are not real.

Now, back in 1989, Kevin asked Roxanne if I had any insurance from my other employment, which I did. He said that I was not in any condition to work. I was saying things like my boss was being unrealistic with me but that was not the truth at all. This was when I received my third impairment charge. My boss, however, kept me on as an employee. That goes to show my aptitude for mechanics. I am not the best but I was skilled and I was constantly learning. (Everyone in the trades does not like to show others new tricks because they are afraid for their own positions, in my opinion.) I ended up at the Down South Mental Health Facility.

I also made a tape recording back then about my fears about bikers and stuff about people who were after me. It was all about my paranoia. Today, I am not sure who some of those people are. I brought the tape to an officer and he automatically knew that I was having some sort of mental breakdown. They called an ambulance for me and checked if I had any weapons, which I did. I had a large machete with the blades sharpened on each side. Lawanda was just a baby and, in my eyes, I was protecting her from what the hallucinations were saying. I never had a thought of harming my children or my wife.

The hallucinations were so intense. The voices sounded like criminals out in the bush; like Freddie Krueger was coming out of the bush after me. I was hearing voices and having to test myself, having to go outside of the house at 3 a.m. because the hallucinations are telling me to come outside and meet someone, because they want to kill me. Could you imagine how horrified I was?

Kevin had been right. I could not work anymore. I ended up at the Down South Mental Health Facility which was the regional mental health facility for that catchment area. I told the doctors about my phobias of bikers and criminal elements—it was all too much to bear. When you are in a place where people are not thinking correctly, it is kind of scary. Staff were always there and they were using different drugs on me. Some drugs were not good and they had many side effects. Haldol was not good for me; there were side-effects like lockjaw.

I was placed on 'forms' to prevent harm to myself or anyone else. People are formed left and right. Forms allows the government to hold you without release from hospital. You are not a voluntary patient, you are 'committed'. It is hard to keep myself together every day, but I still have enough sense to know that if I need to be admitted that I do because it is about my safety and that of others. I find it very degrading to have the government state that they are going to look at you for whatever period of time that they choose. I feel badly for myself that I have to endure a mental illness. It is unfortunate, but I have to follow the laws of the medical sector.

I don't remember how long I stayed at the hospital this time. I know I was in the acute care ward, so I was not there long-term. Sometimes it is difficult to remember the time frames but what I am dictating is all to the best of my abilities.

We all have life struggles; there is no machine that will cure us. There are no cures for any illness, there are only treatments. The doctors that I have dealt with recently have been quite gracious. I have been dealing with them for a number of years. They know me and understand what is and is not part of my illness, and I have managed to control it.

Roxanne and my girls were never homeless. We had some nice places and I still worked. People knew me in Battle Sound and they always had jobs for me. Back home from the hospital, I tried to rehabilitate myself at the Help Centre. Ms. J and Ms. L were people who ran the Help Centre and they set me up with jobs, like mowing lawns and such. Drew was my psychoanalyst. I showed him an article that I wrote in the paper about understanding schizophrenia. So I started a self-help group for people that were mentally ill called Understanding Schizophrenia (U.S.). We met every third Thursday of the month. There were quite a few people that came out.

Roger came over with his wife Marie and their boy Troy. Roger and I worked at Strongman's together. I showed him the article in the Battle Sound newspaper about my self-help group. Roger immediately felt that he had to leave and take his wife and child with him. I thought that he would understand, but he did not. Schizophrenia is not a virus, it is not an airborne disease. It might be hereditary, but you cannot catch it.

Roger had been my friend. Before I was ill, back at Strongman's, I told Devon, my boss, that we should send the fuel injection pump for calibration. He said that it would be OK without it. They put it back to work, against my advice, and the governor snapped on it. Roger told me the exhaust on that Ford diesel turned red hot, but it did not blow up. When the governor goes, the engine over-revs. Roger came over to my side and he called me "Doctor", which was my nickname. He said that I really did a good job at putting that together. I was hurt that he took his friendship away from me.

I really wish that I could go back to work. I now sit alone in my apartment talking into a tape recorder to write this book. Living with schizophrenia is horrendous. I would love to go back to work, but my thinking is not clear, my thoughts race. To go back into mechanics is dangerous. My mind is always racing. I cannot drive a car anymore, either. I would get into an accident trying to get out of a parking lot. I had to surrender my driver's license to the police in 2005.

In 1989, I had a new start, with new people and new places. There was Doris, secretary for the Help Centre. Drew was a psychoanalyst. Then my doctor at that time was Alan. He took care of the people in Battle Sound. I had made a friend at the South Bay Psychiatric Hospital. His name was Wayne. Wayne suffered from bipolar disorder. We shared our life stories. Roxanne and I were good friends of Wayne. Then I started self-help groups. The second one was U.M.I., which stood for Understanding Mental Illness. It was held every third Thursday of the month. I would hold meetings in a church basement. I joked around with U.M.I. as if to say, "Who am I?" When I changed the name from U.S. to U.M.I., more people came. The people who knew me in Battle Sound knew I was having a hard time. I attended the Lord's Hall in Battle Sound for my spirituality and I liked going there because the people were kind and friendly.

I wish that the illness would leave me. To jump back to 1985, in the hospital they put me into seclusion because I had so much paranoia.

I knew that no one could get me in there, no one could hurt me. I felt relief. The staff were good to me because I was not out to hurt anybody. (Not to say I was perfect by any means, I could be tough if need be.) I have never taken anyone's life. Like the forms for self-harm or to hurt someone else, it is a precaution. So in the hospital you can let the medications work, get better and then return home.

(Is it time for a cigarette yet? It is 7:15. Talking about smoking, I believe that people with mental illness smoke because it helps them. The doctors say that smoking cuts the effects of the medication, that if you did not smoke you could probably increase your mental status. Someday I will try to quit again, and that is pretty much for that.)

While in Battle Sound, I met the director of the District Health Council. These health councils directed the hospitals. The woman that ran it was Kim. The government at that time in the 1990s wanted to hear from the consumers as to what to do. Since I had my self-help groups, Kim brought me on board to go to a conference in Large Town. We spent a few nights at the Holiday Inn on King Street. I attended all of the workshops. There were all kinds of people there: professional people, government people and, most importantly, people suffering from mental illness. As you can tell, I am proactive regarding mental illness. It has distorted my life to such an extent and is a day-to-day struggle.

Drew, the psychoanalyst, got into a problem in Battle Sound. He was diagnosing three-quarters of his patients with multiple personality disorder. He ran himself into a lot of hot water. I believe it was *The Fifth Estate* that ran the story and exposed him. He was a kind and gentle man, just trying to help people the best he could. Unfortunately for him things became a little bit sour. Things like this happen. We are dealing with a profession that has its ups and downs. He was sued by approximately seven or eight clients. In this business there is bound to be mistakes made. There was only one perfect one and we hung him 2,000 years ago.

* * *

I think we live in a very weird time here. I am on Mill Street, right beside the jail, in a group home for the time being. It has been my home for approximately six-and-a-half years. I do not sit outside at nighttime. I do not even like to go outside after nine o'clock because you have people on the street yelling and screaming at each other. Not like they are getting into fights or anything like that. I did not realize it would ever be like this. It is so intense with people, and tensions are mounting. We are dealing with all kinds of wars overseas and it is such a depressing atmosphere for anyone on the planet.

My positive inner voice is what keeps me alive. Unlike the auditory hallucinations, my inner voice instructs me not to give up, saying *it is going to get better, do not think of suicide, do not worry—heaven and hell will take care of themselves.* I suppose those expressions are my guiding light because it would be so simple for me to just give up and end my life. But how would my daughters feel if I did that, how would my ex-wife feel if I did that, how would people that know me feel like, how would they feel if I was to do that? I would simply become a statistic like my older brother Danny. I do not want to give up, even though for the last six years I have had unexplainable body pains, back pains, and shooting pains through my legs to the point that walking is difficult. They have given me MRIs (Magnetic Resonance Imaging), they have given me CAT scans (Computer Aided Tomography), they have done a Doppler Ultrasound and finally an Aorta ultrasound.

It took three years of testing to find out how big this aneurysm is. Yes, it is an abdominal aortic aneurysm. I am glad that the doctors found it. It started out at 3.5 centimeters. Two years later it has grown to 4.8-4.9 centimeters. When it gets to 5.5 centimeters, they will have to operate. This is good because I do not want to go in for an operation on my heart for the aorta right away.

It is amazing that I am suicidal at times. I do not want to do it, obviously, but I do have suicidal ideations. It worries me so much that my physical health is failing. I get uptight when I talk to specialists, even before I talk to them. My anxiety is so high that I have fits of diarrhea, and most of the time I am constipated due to the drug Clozaril and all the other medications, such as anti-psychotics, antidepressants and mood stabilizers.

I was at Saint Francis Medical Center getting the tests done and I was really having a difficult time with the anxiety but the Triple Trees Hospital was so kind enough to let me stay in hospital. Three weeks passed by while they were checking my heart. This was at the end of 2009 when I had to go through those stressful events due to my aorta.

I have been quoted as being, "high-functioning", which is good, I guess, since some people are in much more dire straits than I am. I just want to help people and that is why I am doing this, recording my story, for the better mental health of all.

* * *

Over at Madd Avenue in Battle Sound, before my hospital visit in 1989, I am not having any visual hallucinations, but I am a frozen to the kitchen chair and I am looking out of the window and the voices are saying, "It is time to kill you". *Are there people hiding behind the buildings?* Again, this paranoia was due to my 1985 encounter with some people who I do not even consider as 'people', due to what they did to me back then.

Remember, I got into a big mess back in 1985 during my jail term. I did not know what to think. Everybody was on pins and needles then; it was so heavy-duty you could look it up in the *Normalville Star* newspaper. It was such a big trial, with a lot of Ontario Provincial Police, Large Town police, and jail guard involvement. We heard later that the jail had been bugged to get evidence on the accused. The defence lawyers were stating that the bugging was not even legal, not constitutional. The integrity of the jail was breached when the bikers were able to accost me from outside during the trial. It was a whole mess and something that really messed up my life because it gave me paranoia and psychosis. I have not even started telling you about my psychosis yet, but do not worry, I will be talking to you about it.

During the year of 1990 or 1991, Roxanne, the two girls and myself all moved back down to Normalville, Ontario. Roxanne, my wife then, was of the opinion that I needed to live closer to the hospital, meaning Triple Trees. While in Battle Sound, I had had admissions at the Down

South Mental Health Center and admissions at the South Bay Psychiatric Hospital, both of them out-of-town. I had to realize that the rest of my life would be impacted by this disease, unlike back in 1985, when I was able to walk it off. It took me about six months, but I walked off the auditory hallucinations and I ended up getting employment again in Battle Sound.

Back in 1985, I walked it off. It was great. I was functioning again and I had returned back to work. Like I said, I walked it off and I had a lot of strong spiritual beliefs. I believed that God had the power to heal and, in 1985, he did. However, in 1989, when I became ill again and I wanted to walk it off, I couldn't. I wish that a person could just walk it off, but that was not the case this time.

When your dopamine and serotonin receptors are not working right, you are chemically unbalanced. The medications are trying to rebalance that. Lucky for me, at the present time, I have just gotten out of the hospital approximately two weeks ago. I spent three weeks in the hospital and Dr. B put me on Invaga and it is smarting me right up. My awareness is better, my concentration is better, my train of thought is good, my memory seems to be better and hopefully I have just started to find a new neuroleptic that is only a year-old in Canada that has been used in the States. It is very good; it is doing a wonderful job on me, so like I said, day in and day out, that is all I can do. That is all anybody can do.

We live in different times. I never realized when I was going to school that the world would shape out to the way it is. It has always been a constant challenge with people. I wholeheartedly believe that the Lord has put us on this earth for a reason and my reason being is to help out other people who are suffering from mental disorders and to try to break down the stigma, like I mentioned before. (I do not mean to repeat myself over and over but I am telling my story as it comes. I am not reading any scripts or anything; I simply sit here with the pause button, on and off, as I come up with ideas and the history of my life. Hopefully, I can go somewhere with this.)

If you recall, my daughter Lawanda was born in Battle Sound, and after she was a couple of years old, we were living on Rabbit Trail Road. I was hearing voices every day by this time.

There were approximately three different voices talking to me and talking amongst themselves. I could recognize three different vocal ranges. Often, during this time, I would be in the basement, petrified, just scared out of my mind listening to them. Especially with all the basement windows, there I would be thinking things like, *Oh, they are going to break through that window and come and get me, dismember me, kill me, and take my family away.* It just went on and on. I was too scared to cut the lawn, because there were people out in the bush waiting to get me. I would try to sleep on the couch but was unable to do so. I would have insomnia when the girls and Roxanne were in the house. I would try to listen to music to calm my nerves. I used to like rock and roll, such as Bon Jovi, Led Zeppelin, Pink Floyd and basically all the great bands of the late seventies and early eighties. But it was scary in the basement—I was terrified. You can imagine the toll that takes on your body, your body constantly having worrisome thoughts like that and the paranoia.

I would wake up at three a.m.—I do not know if you would really call it waking up since I had not slept—and I would challenge the voices by going outside to find them out. *Are they really out there? Are they actually saying these things to me?* And I would finally realize that they were not. *There is nobody out there, Allan, there is nobody out there.* Why was this happening to me? To walk down secluded Rabbit Trail Road at night and be in this totally different mindset, it would be enough to frighten anybody. It is a wonder why I did not have all these fits of diarrhea due to anxiety, auditory hallucinations and delusions that my life was in danger.

Now, here I sit in my group home and I think that the staff are in some sort of plot, or that the other tenants are in on some sort of plot to hurt me, or that I messed up the wrong people in 1985. I did not mess up anybody in 1985, and if the jail had been bugged, I did not put the bugs in there.

* * *

Well, I just finished my laundry today. That is what I do at the group home; we all have our chores. I live with seven other people that are affected with mental illness. I have been here approximately five years. The Canadian

Mental Health Association (CMHA) has staff at the home from one in the afternoon until six in the evening. There are usually two staff here during those times to assist us with our everyday chores. I would like to get out of the group home and get into a single dwelling—or a double dwelling with a girlfriend. It would be a good thing. It is rough, though, the problem being that if you need the services offered at the group home later, you have to re-apply and get on the waiting list again.

It is quite the big jump to move out on your own or to live with someone else. It is not that bad of a place here. The common living area is nice, the living room area is nice and we are all polite to each other. We all know that we have our troubles. I like joking around with the staff and the other tenants and it is a lot of fun sometimes. There is always something to do, we have resources, a recovery board listing all the facilities and different places that have something for us to do. It is truly a good thing.

Then, every Wednesday I go to the drug clinic at Triple Trees. My advice to anyone is that, if you know you need the help, find it. If you need the extra supports, find them. It is too hard to do it on your own. I cannot imagine a person doing it on their own. Then again, I might be mistaken in saying that, in that other people probably do function quite well individually.

I am going to talk about the group home a bit more (I was talking into the microphone and the record button had not been pushed, so there you go, I am not perfect, that is for sure). Anyway, I share the group home with seven other tenants who have mental illnesses and we all have our chores to do. Every Monday, I cook with Barry and he helps put out cups and stir the juice and that. I try to cook nutritious meals: I am pretty famous for my tuna salad sandwiches and my egg salad sandwiches.

Oh yes, living beside the Normalville District Jail, what a treat that is! Sometimes the other tenants and I joke about having to live beside the jail—that it is the jail's outreach program for people suffering with mental illness—but it is a place to live, so that is a good thing. On Mill Street there are other buildings, some of them are apartment buildings, but we are the ones closest to the jail. One of the nurses that I know from the Triple Trees hospital also works at the jail. I talk to her. I talk to the guards sometimes, too. Life is life, people are people, that is all I can say about that.

Well, at least I have a place to stay. In the Normalville area there are approximately eight hundred people that are homeless and that is quite the high number. These issues need to be addressed. We live in Canada. One of the richest countries in the world.

I would say, fifteen to twenty years ago, some of the students coming out of our universities were top-notch, best in the world. Canada has so much to offer the world. I believe politicians do make mistakes, but the thing is, I have just finished filling out Ontario Common Assessment of Needs (OCAN), a collaboration between CMHA and myself and the other tenants. The government is looking at the needs of people with mental illness and hopefully something will come of this. I think that was a major undertaking of the government. There are a lot of resources out there. It is just that you have to go out and find them because they are there. Maybe there were more of them ten years ago, a decade ago. Things are shrinking because of the economy being in such rough shape. I believe peer support networks are coming into play due to the fact that the government does not have much money for formal mental health facilities. So 'warm lines' are becoming necessary, so people suffering from mental health issues can talk to others with mental health issues who have a good understanding.

Sometimes at the group home I think we are dealing with a poltergeist, but obviously we are not. Those are some of the things that go through my mind, like when I hear noises that are unexplained, or we have a leaky fridge. Nothing has spilled inside of it the fridge, but it leaks on the floor. The stove temperature is hard to regulate. Sometimes I hear voices talking to the other tenants, "Boy, we have a real winner here, eh?" Sometimes I say to myself, *What is the matter—you do not believe in haunted houses.* I related that to Dr. M, who was my psychiatrist while I was in the hospital and she said to me, "I do not believe in haunted houses." That gave me relief.

*   *   *

Now I want to talk about my father, whom I loved very much. I remember when I was just a baby. We were driving somewhere when our truck broke down and he had to walk halfway from Normalville to Hill Top to pick up a fuel pump or something. I do not know the details as I was just a baby then. I do not know what year that truck was, either, but my family does have pictures and photographs.

My dad put in seven years in the Second World War as a bulldozer operator, and that was quite the thing. He did not really talk about the war much. I guess it was too much to even think about, let alone talk about.

After the truck, the next car my father had was a 1957 Plymouth Fury, and he had that for quite a number of years. The next car he had was a 1966 Plymouth Valiant, with a 225 slant six engine in it. Back then in 1973, he could afford a brand new Plymouth Valiant with a 318 C.I.D. (cubic inch displacement) engine in it, and that was his first new car.

Then he bought himself a Pontiac Acadian and that was approximately in 1984, which, sadly, was the vehicle he was killed in. Yes, it was a Pontiac Acadian 1984. I went to the wrecking yard to look at it, it was a mess. It was T-boned by a gentleman driving a station wagon while he was trying to get his child to school. It just goes to show you that you never really know, do you.

Now that I think about it, my dad did talk about the Second World War every once in a while. He mentioned to me a point where they were running through the fields and the Germans were bombing them quite heavily. A friend right beside him was hit with a very large shell and just disappeared. He was vaporized.

Like I said, my father was driving bulldozers and one of the large shells that the Germans had locked onto him. They made a very weird noise before they impacted with anything. He heard it coming, so he hid underneath the back-end of the bulldozer. The bulldozer's blade was directly hit, but he survived. I do not know why it did not deafen him.

My father spent seven years in the Small Town Volunteer Fire Department. He was quite the guy. Muscular and able to work at MEN Mining for 36 years, and a volunteer fireman for seven years. He was involved in the Legion for the veterans of the Second World War. Because he was a veteran, he came up and saw me working for the Department of National

Defense, where I was rebuilding a very large diesel engine at the radar base in Normalville.

Yes, I can tell you the story of how my mom and dad met. They were working for Blackman's down near Center Lake in Normalville, Ontario. The Blackmans used to own Blackman's department stores. After the Second World War, my dad had gone to Large Town and worked a little bit there in a chocolate factory. He could not stand it because everyone was spitting into the chocolate. His sister, Gem, my Aunt Gem, was living in Normalville with her husband at the time, Dean. My dad moved from Large Town and lodged at his sister's place in Normalville. My dad was working at Blackman's when he met my mom. She was like a maid to the Blackman's and my father was their groundskeeper. My dad was 31 years of age and my mom was 18. And so they got together. My father only had a Grade 8 education and I believe that my mom had her Grade 12. After they were married they had an apartment in Normalville and during the first seven years my dad worked graveyard shift at MEN Mining checking for loose rock.

My parents got married and then they had Danny in January 1951, soon after they married.

My dad later found a house in Hill Top and bought it through the Veterans Land Act, more commonly known as the VLA. The next-door neighbors were the Players. Fred Player knew my dad from the Second World War and so when Mr. Player saw my dad first roll in on a motorcycle, he said, "Well, hello there, Motorcycle Man."

I loved my father very, very much and I loved my mother very, very much. At times I gave them a hard time, but that is what growing up is all about.

* * *

My dad was born in a place called Naple, up north in Saskatchewan. His family had a farm out there, 460 acres. It also had a lake on it. When I was 17 years of age, I had the opportunity to see it. My dad went and bought himself a small, compact Triple-E trailer and we used the 1973 Valiant to pull it. Therefore, we did not have to worry about paying for motels or hotels. We got into a little trouble from Normalville to Thomas Bay, Ontario. When we reached Thomas Bay we were having an overheating problem, so we had to stop at a scrap yard and changed the radiator. The radiator came from a 340 C.I.D. high-performance Dodge engine. We straightened up that problem on our way to Saskatchewan, and then we got into another little problem with the suspension holding up the trailer. It was a Reese trailer-hitch and we had to reinforce the rear shocks with external spring kits. (Hopefully, this is not too boring for people who are not mechanically inclined or anything, but the reason why I speak of it is in order to tell you some of my experiences that I had in my career life.)

Back then at 17 years of age, I was out of high school due to quitting at age 16. I went down to Saskatchewan with my kid sister, mom and dad. It was quite the adventure. When my family went back home, I stayed in Saskatchewan at the Salvation Army.

During my stay at the Sally Ann I ended up partying here and there with the other people. At 17 I was partying it up, drinking underage and living quite the life. Looking back at it now, it was just like self-medicating or something in order to deal with all my emotional problems.

The Salvation Army put me up at this place called The Champ Hotel and everyone there was on welfare. I was not really a vagrant, I did work out there. I was washing dishes, but I ended up getting punched out at The Champ Hotel. It was my own fault. I was bragging about knowing something about karate and this guy wanted to prove to me that I did not know anything about it, so he ended up punching me out quite nicely. Talk about learning your lesson well.

The bus ride back home was three days and during that time I ate absolutely nothing. When I finally got back home to Hill Top in Normalville, I ate a pound of bacon, a loaf of bread and a dozen eggs. My mom built me up again and fed me well.

That is when I had to start working shoveling asphalt. Quite the job that was, every day, day in and day out. I kept saying to myself, "If I can make it through another day, just give me another day, just give me another day." It is pretty hard to look into the future when you are pretty certain that you may take your own life. It is not a funny thing at all. There is nothing amusing about it in the least. That is one of the reasons why I had so many hospitalizations, like when I started having my psychotic episodes in 1985.

I have to say it was due to all the external pressures and events that caused me to have very bad and serious breakdowns. There is a song by the Barenaked Ladies, "If I Had $1,000,000"; if I had a million dollars, I would certainly spend it on mental health patients. One thing they could probably use is a new TV in their hospital rooms.

Let us talk about my mother. She was very young and had a very strong French character. She was the disciplinarian in the family and would tell you which way was up, while my dad was very soft-spoken. My mom was the eldest child, followed by her siblings Cathy and Tommy. My mom worked at a confectionary store near Old Street. She grew up at 75 Old Street in Normalville. My mother liked to roller skate, go bowling, and cook. Above all, she was a very good mother. I would have to say my parents were almost blameless. They were not alcoholics, abusers or addicts. The only bad thing you could say they did was smoke cigarettes.

Her mother, my grandmother, I knew very well. After elementary school I would spend the summers with my grandmother, which was nice. She would spoil me, but I guess that is what grandmothers are for. The Normalville District Housing authority housed my grandmother on Light Street. This is when they tore down all of the old markets and put the Complex Shopping Center there. They also built the Ukrainian church on Stills Avenue. Yes, Normalville was on the move.

Now I could talk about my younger sister Lynn. Unfortunately, she has multiple sclerosis now. It is hard and I wish I knew more about MS. I guess I could read up more on it. Actually, a month ago there was something on the television about it. Something about them finding genes and nerve endings where it can alleviate paralysis, I would imagine. That would be nice.

Lynn was quiet as a child, and even now. How she loved animals! I remember she had hamsters as a kid. There were dogs and cats and at least one rabbit in our house, as I recall. Lynn became a veterinary assistant. The MS has not keep her from her love of working with animals. She still works.

Then we had our younger brother Bobby. He was versed in St. John's ambulance training. After Grade 12, at Saint Paul College, he did two years of college, taking instrument mechanics and computers. Currently he is working in Ottawa and has done very well for himself.

After my mom's death in 2004, we all split up with a little bit of money and sold my mother's house in Hill Top. With his share, Bobby bought himself a Yamaha Warrior. I believe it was a 1700 CC's engine.

I try to keep in contact with Bobby, Lynn, Lawanda and Melanie and through e-mail. I e-mail them and they e-mail me back. It is good that I still have my girls and I still have my ex-wife Roxanne, whom I still talk to over the phone. You know, after 25 years of marriage you get to know the in's and out's of that person very well. It is so unfortunate; I miss my ex-wife and I wish that would have never happened. I will tell you what happened.

The thing was, back in January of 2005, things were not going well. Roxanne was not treating me well at all. I had to stay in the basement, I had to sleep in the basement, I was not allowed to smoke in the house and I could not use the computers.

There was no physical harm on either side. She never hurt me and I never hurt her but I did phone the crisis service once, and during that call, I said that I wanted to commit suicide and that I wanted to murder my wife. Which I did not do, but the police came and I was charged with uttering a death threat. I did not realize that was against the law, but it is. You cannot threaten the life of anyone. You cannot be ignorant of the law and, just because you do not know that a particular law is there, it does not mean you will not get charged with it. I paid dearly for that. I was incarcerated and checked into the South Bay Psychiatric Hospital in the forensics unit. I was evaluated in order to see if I was stable enough to be out in society. I was.

What I had to go through was totally horrible. I suppose it was also horrible for Roxanne. I just wish we could have seen eye-to-eye but we did not and when our marriage disintegrated, I just about lost it. I do not hold any resentment toward the police, the parole board or the people that I was involved with in 2005, and everything is now cleared. I made a mistake and, as they say, you learn from your mistakes. You certainly do learn, it is true.

It had been a hard time for me and Roxanne in the years before our breakup. My mother had suffered from brain cancer on the left hemisphere of her brain. She had a small spot of cancer and it took about five-and-a-half months until she subsided to it, in early 2005. Families and funerals, unfortunately, often bring on family feuds due to the emotional stress. Roxanne was made executor to my mom's estate and in the will it was stated that the estate was to be divided equally between Lynn, Bobby and myself. Even before my mother's death, my family was upset that Roxanne was executor. My uncle, who is married to my mother's sister Cathy, went down to the bank and tried to change the will so that he could be executor. Nobody agreed that I should have a third of her estate. I still do not understand why, but to Roxanne and I, it was so messed up. She could not take the stress anymore. I think that is when our marriage ended, even though we were still married for three more years. The break-up of my family is something I totally regret. At this point, I try to forgive and forget.

I am good and honest at heart, but the things Roxanne had to go through to make sure that things were divided equally was unbelievable. During this time I had to leave college, where I was upgrading, and one thing happened after another. It was very painful for me. After my mom's death I stayed at her house for 18 months trying to sell it. We did not ask much for it, about 42,000 dollars. It was a nice two-bedroom house in Hill Top Heights with a garage and also another part of a large property. My parents had bought two properties through the VLA. It was a great area. Later, I actually saw the house on the real estate channel. The people who bought it fixed it up and were now asking 142,000 dollars for it. That was the place I was born and raised.

I have to say, if you have come this far with me, with my book or through my tapes, you might be asking yourself, "Who does this guy think he is?" Well, I am just Allan Jones, that is who I am. I am just another human being like everyone else on Planet Earth. The thing is, I am just telling you my life and how it has been impacted by all kinds of traumatic events. Sure, some could have been avoided, but it all comes out in the wash, as they say. I have made mistakes just like everybody else has and I have rectified them, thank God for that. I will make sure that there is some way that people can share their input with me as to what they think of my life story up to the age of 54. I would welcome anyone's opinion about it.

* * *

Let us step it up a bit, let us talk about psychotic episodes. They are caused by delusions, auditory hallucinations and a break with reality. Now, as I have said, I live right beside the district jail. One night, in January or March of 2009, in the middle of the night, I got up and, oh, I was having really bad auditory hallucinations. They were telling me to bolt out in front of traffic (which I did not do), telling me to wait at the side of the road because someone was going to pick me up in an old Cadillac. I was up and down the stairs of the house, back and forth between my room and the door, I was so scared. Some of the tenants were downstairs and I should have told them I was having a psychotic episode and that the voices were really bad. How I survived it, I do not know. It was nighttime; I was freezing cold and wrapped around a little portable heater that I have in my room. I could hear bikers accusing me of blowing up their clubhouse. I was cold and I was running up and down the stairs. I was waiting in the porch for someone to come up to the door and take me away and throw me in the trunk and do a massive burnout. I went outside and stayed there close to an hour, with no boots in depth of winter.

The episode was quite severe and I should have just told some of the other tenants what I was going through, but I did not because I thought that they were all in on it, even though it is obvious now that they were not. So, anyways, I was hearing voices saying, "We have lost two good police officers because of you!" It was not true—I was having auditory hallucinations, delusions and a severe psychotic episode. I was in fear for my life. So I listened to the commanding voices. "We're going to bring you in right now," they said. I went outside. "We're not going to shoot you." I walked up to one of the steel doors at the jail. I was holding myself up real steady. I thought that the police had guns aimed on me. I stood there thinking that people were making fun of me, and I heard an old police car siren sounding off in the background.

Here I was, at this steel door, waiting for the guards of the jail to come and get me. I stood there for twenty minutes before the police finally showed up and asked me what I was doing there. I frantically told them that I thought I may have just killed someone. The police took me to Saint Francis Hospital right away, where a doctor assessed me. I was discharged the next day. They did not, I believe, even write me up. That was a severe psychotic episode. The next day I had to go grocery shopping and I was completely exhausted.

It is completely out of this world for someone to go through something like that. Like, should this person really be out in society? I even have to question that and question myself. But, as long as I keep my cool and do not hurt anyone (including myself), everything will be fine. I tell you, when you have schizophrenia, it is something else.

If I could only get through to the young people today about first psychosis. The first time you experience something like that, you need to tell your parents or foster parents or whatever the situation might be. You need direct medical intervention because you do not want to hurt yourself or someone else. Your mind is racing a million thoughts a second.

It is so unbelievable what a chemical imbalance can do to a person. I imagine that some of the police must think I am some sort of head case. Well, that is an unfortunate thing to say and I should not even be using words like that. People suffering from mental illnesses are simply people suffering from mental illnesses.

Like I have said to the helping professionals and the doctors and clinicians I have dealt with, I would rather take my own life before taking anyone else's life and that is the absolute truth. I have never hurt anyone, I am just trying to live a normal life and it is hard to live a normal life when you are not feeling well.

What I am seeing in psychiatric hospitals today is a revolving door for a lot of people. They go in with serious problems and then they are discharged way before they get well. I believe back in the late eighties and early nineties that a patient's stay was probably longer than what it is today. It seems as though it is a funding problem with the Ontario Hospital Insurance Plan, otherwise known as OHIP.

Unfortunately, our government is talking about private health care and hopefully our hospital system does not turn into what the United States hospital system is like. Hopefully we do not have to experience that, hopefully public hospitals will be open to everyone who is in need of medical services.

OK, time to tell you about another psychotic episode that happened during January or March of 2005. I was staying at my friends' place (Blaine and Lisa's) in order to make sure that I would attend my court hearing regarding my charge for uttering a death threat. At the time, Blaine and Lisa were just living a couple of houses down from my mother's old house, which we had just sold. Listening to my voices, I walked away from Blaine and Lisa's house. While I was in the house, the voices had been saying that Officer Friendly was outside waiting for me to come out peacefully, and that Dr. John was also out there waiting for me to come out. They were apparently going to place me under arrest. For what, I do not know. The voices and the delusions were so horrific that I just went outside of the house. I was hearing instructions, like "Lie down on the ground with your hands behind your head," which I did. They were not necessarily voices, but commanding auditory hallucinations. I lay down on the ground near my mother's house for approximately 45 minutes on Highway 96. It was March, and it was freezing cold. Cars just drove by, and no one stopped.

A friend from across the street came up to me and said, "Allan, what are you doing?" He offered to help me back inside the house. I said to him, "No, just leave me out here." With that, he just left, and I still lay there. He must have wondered what the heck was going on with his friend who he had known all of his life. Here I was, lying down in the freezing snow and slush, in March.

Finally, Lisa returned home to discover me on the road. She drove up and said, "Allan, get into the house right now." I did. I pleaded with her not to tell Blaine about the episode. Despite this, Lisa told Blaine that I was really sick.

There was another episode, too. I do not want to have to bore anyone but when things like this are happening to you, you need direct intervention. How I did it without direct intervention, I do not know. When you have stuff like that happening to you, you need help. It is as simple as that, and it seems to me that the further along I go, I improve myself. So I hope that I can make you understand the severity of auditory hallucinations and delusional thinking.

There are a lot of times I ask myself and the doctors whether I need a long-term care facility, because people having psychotic episodes like this are totally not to blame. (Just as a side note, could you imagine someone standing at the door of the jail, waiting to be brought in, even though they have not done anything wrong? I really try to keep on the humorous side of it all.)

There is just so much stuff happening out there today. I do not even know what to think at times. The way society is today, it is an unfortunate thing, you know. I think, because of it, people are becoming more dissociated with each other. The computer age is here, people are spending more time with technology. The divorce rate is increasing. People are disheartened about the work they are doing. People are losing their jobs left and right.

Hopefully good will come out of all of this. Hopefully mankind can suffice.

I have an old friend by the name of Joe. He lives in Normalville. We went to diesel mechanic school together and I stop to talk to him once in a while. He is all right and sometimes he asks me how I am doing. I say I am doing just fine, as I often say to everyone else; meanwhile, I am feeling pretty sick. I do not feel well at all most of the time, but I keep going on. I keep on trying to do my best. It is too bad we cannot just wave a magic wand and make things all better again. *You are OK, you are healed! Yes, everything is going to be all right.* You cannot just sweep it under the carpet. I have always said to myself: we have the alcoholics in the basement, the homosexuals in the closet and the mentally ill in the attic. That is the way society treated people back then and, unfortunately, that is the way they treat people today.

We have people with different diseases coming forward with their ailments, like Michael J. Fox, who has Parkinson's disease. I think that the people of the world have to step forward and say, "Look at me, I have this ailment." Society should be made aware of all the contributions that people have made to the understanding of mental illness. Society should know about mental illness. The people suffering from it should let other people who are, let us say, "normal", know about the trials and tribulations of mental illness. I would love to break the stigma. Centuries ago people were burned at the stake for being different. They were called heretics and it goes on and on to the sanitariums of the 1900s which were nothing more than prisons.

There are a number of movies that have transpired over the years that reduce stigma. "A Beautiful Mind" with Russell Crowe comes to mind. We need more movies like that, such as "One Flew Over the Cuckoo's Nest" with Jack Nicholson, "Girl Interrupted" with Winona Ryder and Angelina Jolie, "What About Bob" with Bill Murray, and "The Soloist" with Jamie Foxx. When I think about these films, I find them based more in fact than fiction.

I have shared my story publicly. Three years ago, in 2010, I described my life and experiences with mental illness in a video produced by the local Canadian Mental Health

Association. I also wrote a piece for another CMHA publication. In 1998, I was also published in the *Canadian Journal of Occupational Therapy*. Carol interviewed me. I said that I just wanted to be a someone. When you are not feeling well everything else just takes a backseat. When I am using the services I need, I feel bad about spending the government's money. But like the doctors told me, if it was not you, it would just be someone else. Something I just found out is that 1 in every 5 people suffer from a mental illness. Those are pretty staggering numbers. One in 100 people have schizophrenia.

We have to debunk the stigma of mental illness. We hear: *People who are mentally ill are violent and dangerous, totally out there to get everyone! Oh scary, scary—do not talk to that one, he is sick and you might catch it! Do not go there, she has it!* What a bunch of hogwash. I have read some books, and E. Fuller Torrey's, *Surviving Schizophrenia* is a great book. In it, he states that he would rather walk the halls of a mental institution at midnight rather than the streets of New York.

I struggle, too, when I see people who have bipolar, schizophrenia and eating disorders, among other things. There is nothing as sad as a girl with an eating disorder that thinks she is overweight when she is skin and bones. I have seen a lot of women with that disease. It is a shame.

My mother had post-partum depression for my younger brother Bobby in 1972 and she had to go through horrible things such as a E.C.T. (electroconvulsive therapy), drug therapy and the like. Dr. John at one time told me that post-partum depression comes out of thin air. When I was born in Normalville, Ontario, in 1958, my mother had to be transported to the South Bay Psychiatric Facility and at that time it was a jail. There were killers in there: baby killers, husband killers and so on. It is so unfortunate that women come down with a disease like post-partum depression. If untreated, some of these poor women break the law and do things they would normally never do. Some women have just given birth at the time and do not want anything to do with their baby. It is terrible and I just wish science would come up with something to help these women. It was about six months until my mother started getting back on her feet after she had me. I am just going to say jokingly that it was my fault that she had post-partum because I was such a crazy person. (When this project is all complete, I hope that other people will not put me down, if they think I said something that was demeaning to them, I certainly do not mean it to be.)

I went to a Christmas party today put on by the ACTT Team and it was a good thing. I won myself a little present, except the present is for my girls to have. I know most of the health professional workers in the mental illness field in the Normalville area which is good because I can talk openly and they are there to help people.

Our mental health system today has improved, but could still improvise more options to bring us into the twenty-first century. In the meantime, you might not be feeling well, but you know, there are pros and cons to everything. You might not thinking straight and you may need people to help you focus, but hopefully in time, with medication, therapy and with counseling, you will be able to live some sort of life instead of just existing.

I know that your quality-of-life seems to go downhill when you are not feeling well, but fortunately you can make it go uphill for yourself. Get active in reading, woodworking or whatever mental health services have to offer you. Not only are these services helping you, but they are helping your relatives. A lot of relatives are like, "Oh God, what are we going to do?" Mental illness puts such a burden on families and I would imagine that sometimes the burden is too much and that they have to dissociate themselves from the person that is mentally ill. Caregivers burnout, too, and they need to take a break. It is unfortunate, but that is the case.

People are only people, we can only handle so much. You need to carry on, even though there is a lot of confusion, destitution, meagre living and maybe even homelessness. The healthcare system should be revamped in a way that the money is spent positively, in a positive light, and not wasted in duplication of services. I think that everybody has to sit around the table and try to find better solutions to these problems. Professionals and caregivers should weigh all the options available to them and the person suffering from illness. I do not mean to speak ill of the mental health system. We are fortunate that we do not live in a third-world country where there would be no mental health services at all.

* * *

My life has been hard, but I have good memories. Roxanne, the kids and I had nice Christmases. We would always put up a tree and have presents to go around. Even though I would struggle day-in and day-out, I did the best I could with my family, and my girls are now on their way to becoming professionals.

Even today, I have to push myself to function and have as normal a life as possible. In this timeframe, right now in the group home, I constantly use the staff as a sounding board to make sure things are all right, to make sure that I should not be paranoid, to make sure that it is not an elaborate scheme or some sort of mass conspiracy against me and to make sure that I have not created all kinds of problems for myself. I am just a regular person. I have said things that I regret saying but who has not in their relationship with their spouse, girlfriend or boyfriend? I know one thing though, I really do not want to be alone. I want to find myself another love to continue with my life.

Spending so much time, like I have, trying to regain my health, in hospital and out, you learn a lot from the nursing staff, pastoral care, doctors, and patients. Yes, it all rubs off on you. You learn and you learn and you learn. Every time a hospitalization happens, you learn some more. You learn some more coping mechanisms, you learn some more Tai Chi, you learn some more deep-breathing exercises, you learn some more about pharmacology, you learn some more about spirituality, and it is all for the good.

So one of the reasons I am writing all of this is for the simple fact that it will help someone else. I think if we put our collective voices together we will be heard.

Life is too precious to just give it up. Life is too precious for someone to take. Life is too precious to be taken lightly. Life is too precious to be ignored. Life is too precious to not be taken care of. Life is too precious to waste. Life is your life to live to the fullest and that is what I think the meaning of life is.

Edwards Brothers Malloy
Oxnard, CA USA
May 30, 2013